Pitfalls in Sadhana

(Three Sat-sang Talks, February 1987)

M.P. PANDIT

DIPTI

Publishers:
Dipti Publications,
Sri Aurobindo Ashram,
Pondicherry 605002.

First Edition: 1987
Reprint: 1998

Price: **Rs. 15.00**

ISBN: **81–7509–036–7**

Printed at:
All India Press
Kennedy Nagar, Pondicherry 605001.

I

Meditation — Work — Reading

All of us are admittedly interested in sadhana which for us means a dedicated pursuit of the Divine in our daily life. You might ask why there should be pitfalls, let alone downfalls, in a quest of this type. After all, it is something very sacred, a purposeful moving towards God, and there is no reason why there should be pitfalls. A very legitimate question, but the facts are that this world, the whole universe in fact, is organised at present on a basis of ignorance and its extreme consequence, falsehood. We are in the mid-stage of the evolutionary movement and emerging as we have done from Inconscience, Unconsciousness, there is a great hold of Ignorance and its brood over us. And Nature, by which we mean Nature in Ignorance, takes good care to see that her creatures do not go beyond her.

Nature has implanted in everyone certain qualities, habits, which stand in the way of exceeding her, going beyond her reign as it stands. These are called sentinels of Nature. All around us there are these sentinels guarding this territory for the forces of Ignorance, blocking the onward, upward movement. For instance, take conservatism.

Whether it is individual life or social or political life, whenever any measure of lasting benefit is proposed, there is always a resistance from some quarter or other, resistance to change, resistance to progress. We always want to hold back under the plea of the stability of the society, not going too fast and stumbling. There will be specious reasons. Similarly, among individual seekers doubts will arise. Great experiences come, new truths are presented, but the mind asks, "How do you know that they are true? This could be imagination, or even hallucination." So, there is a doubt and doubt is, as you know, a very corroding element. It will allow you to accept nothing, even concrete proofs. It will always raise a question, a note of skepticism. Take any progressive measure, any discipline that seeks to improve the lot of man; there will always be skeptics who will say, 'let us see, it is not going to work'. Now this kind of unintelligent blind resistance to progress is seen not only in the wide world outside, but, as you would have seen, even in our individual spheres. For any ameliorating measure there are always doubters, skeptics and even ill-wishers. These are the sentinels of Nature to guard this kingdom for the lower gods. That is why you will find everywhere traps, pits, and the Mother points out that the greatest tests are not on big occasions, they are hidden in small details. We are always prepared, — at any rate those of us who are well endowed, — to meet the tests on a larger scale, but when these tests hide behind daily circumstances, apparently insignificant turns of life, we are caught unawares. And they are the pitfalls we tend to ignore. They are the pitfalls into which we find ourselves when we least expect it to happen, because they do not draw our attention. We take many things for granted. When temptations arise, we know. We know also what are unspiritual things, we are prepared for them. But when things are hidden around us, we trip.

To begin with, there is a great confusion between means and ends. Means are measures we adopt in order to reach a definite objective. So, means is one thing, end is another. In this effort everybody starts well, but a stage comes when we are so much lost in the process, in the means, that we forget the purpose for which we engage ourselves in it.

For instance, meditation. Meditation is not an end in itself. Meditation is a means to put yourself in tune with a higher or a deeper consciousness. You withdraw your attention from outside and turn it inwards so that you are for the time being freed from external compulsions and you get an opportunity to experience what goes on about you on a higher or a deeper plane. So, meditation is a technique, a very healthy one, to arrive at a state where you are perfectly in tune with the higher consciousness and you no longer need to meditate. There is a state in the life of the seeker, where meditation becomes so natural that he does not need to sit for meditation. The attitude of meditation is in-built in the being, in the outlook, and things go on within a meditative frame. Meditation has served its purpose. Thereafter one does not need to sit for meditation. But it is common to see persons giving undue importance to meditation, even exclusive importance, and meditating for hours and hours together. Mother always warned one not to meditate for hours unless one could not help it, one were captured by a higher movement and had to let oneself go. Be vigilant, never allow yourself to be lost. With many people who meditate for hours, four hours, five hours, nothing changes outside; they luxuriate within themselves, indulge in what is called *rasāsvāda*, taste of bliss, but there is no effect on their nature. Particularly in a yoga like this where change of nature is of prime importance, a stagnant meditation where you just sit and allow things to happen has no meaning. So many lose themselves, lose the direction, but they do not know it. They live under an illusion. Mother calls for brief periods of dynamic meditation in which aspiration and vigilance are active.

Similarly work. Work occupies a very important place in our path. Before Sri Aurobindo, it was the Bhagavadgita that raised the value of work investing it with a spiritual importance. The Gita points out how work which normally produces karma, a binding chain, loses that feature and becomes a means for spiritual liberation, if it is done in a disinterested manner, as a sacrifice to the Divine. Well, Sri Aurobindo and Mother take up from that point and develop it further as a dynamic factor for inner change. Work is the body's worship of the Divine. But what is this work? It is work done without the desire and ego-motive, work done consciously with a spiritual poise, solemnly offered as worship. What do we do when we worship? For the moment we shed all lower movements, baser attractions. Even the bath that you take is a symbol, a confirmation that you have cleansed yourself of all unspiritual elements. And you lose yourself in worship. You commune with God and pour yourself in a flow of your being. If work is to play this role, it has to be done in that manner. Work devoid of a spiritual attitude, spiritual basis, becomes labour. Mother underlines that it becomes just a physical labour. It has consequences of fatigue and the like. Work becomes competitive, a means for aggrandisement, for exploitation, or mechanical, like work done in a factory. But in a spiritual set-up, work has a spiritual significance only if it is constantly accompanied by a relentless consecration, an offering to the Divine, regardless of any other object. Your attention is always on the work, the purpose for which the work is done and why you are doing it. You do not care what will be the result, it is left to the Divine. You do not worry about what others think of you, what are the reactions of those around you. All that you do is to maintain a spiritual attitude, a spiritual concern for the Divine in humanity, when you do the work. Work should be a means for communicating your level of consciousness to those with whom you work and to those to whom the fruits of your work are to go. So the usual worldly considerations cannot exist here. Otherwise work becomes a trap. Work is spiritual as long as the right consciousness is there. You do not think of position, high or low, subordinate or superior. You do not do work to get kudos, to get appreciation from anyone. You do not do work to get a foothold in an organisation but as a privilege, as a valuable aid in the journey. I remember how in the very early days of the Ashram, work was the one thing that was most prized next to the Mother's touch. The moment one took up work given by Mother one felt launched. She always said that when she gave a work she also gave the capacity to carry out the work. I do remember how, though the office hours were fixed in line with the labour laws, sadhaks themselves worked much longer. They would bring the papers home, they would work outside the regular hours and yet they would be always fresh, there would be no sense of fatigue. Mother was to explain later that the onset of fatigue in work is a sign that there is some vitiation in one's attitude to work. Work is meant, among other things, to raise the levels of your consciousness by learning to exert yourself without ego, without motive, which are the normal compulsions for work; in a collective organisation it is intended to bring in human relations a spirit of harmony, an atmosphere of love, mutual caring, each one helping the other. Here starts the key to brotherhood. Fraternity does not happen merely by thinking of it, but through actual exertion. If you can identify yourself with the collectivity, participate in the struggles of others, forgetting yourself for the while, you have entered into the right spirit of work. Now, each one of us has to ask himself, am I doing this work as part of sadhana, or as a routine of daily life or for some extraneous considerations? Work loses its sacred character if it is tied up with other considerations, work remains work. Further we may tend to develop an attachment to work. There are people who want to do the same thing all the 365 days, they will not accept a change which may be necessitated by the interests of the general community. There is an instinctive preference to stick to the same thing. Work becomes a trap.

Work is sacred, work is great, work is spiritual, but it has to be accompanied by the right consciousness, otherwise it becomes a snare. We have seen people working for sixteen hours, eighteen hours and they will boast of it: I am working eighteen hours, these others hardly work for four hours, they go away one hour before the bell rings and so on. By the very utterance of such a statement you lose the value of the work. You are no longer a worker for the Divine. You develop a complex of self-adulation and depreciation of others. This is one illustration of how we mistake the means for the end. Work by itself is not going to take us to the goal. But it prepares the conditions for our advancement, progress on the path, provided it is done in the right spirit.

Similarly, reading. Our masters have written so much. Mother hardly ever wrote, but whatever she spoke, has run into fifteen volumes and more; people are still withholding what she wrote to them, that is another matter. Now reading is meant to enlighten the mind, culture the mind, bathe the mind in the vibrations of great thoughts, higher truths and create in you the aspiration, the zeal to acquire the same experience. It is meant to inspire you, prod you, to educate you. But reading by itself has no spiritual value. Reading has to be related to your daily life. What you read has to be lived. What you study is to be translated into practice. Philosophy, metaphysics, are not spirituality. I may know in great detail the argument in *The Life Divine*; another person who may not know English may be more advanced spiritually than I am, because I am lost in the academic knowledge. I have a complacency that I have read *The Life Divine*, maybe ten times, twelve times. But there is no gainsaying that it is only an intellectual acquisition and that too, provided I have really understood what Sri Aurobindo has written, and made it a part of my mental equipment. Well, it is a learning. It is what is called knowing the Shastra, but unless it is communicated to the various parts of my being and moulds their movements, it has no direct significance, it has no spiritual value.

There are many in our Ashram who do not know English, who have not read anything. But I have known Sri Aurobindo certifying to the capital realisation of some of those sadhikas. He said of one that she had an Upanishadic realisation. She did not know a word of English. She had only opened herself to Sri Aurobindo. The pride of reading, the vanity of learning is a calamity. People think of the *Mahāvākyas* in the Upanishads, *tat tvam asi*, — That thou art, — *sarvam khalvidam brahma* — All this is Brahman, *ayam ātmā brahma* — This self is Brahman. Sri Ramana Maharshi, the sage of Arunachala, points out that these are only conceptual formulations; they are a mould for your mind to work with but you do not stop there; if you are satisfied with only a mental impact, it stops there. By saying I am He, I do not become He. Once my mind accepts the truth that I am He, I have to use it as a key to open the lock of the inner realm. It should be a starting point, a springboard; then alone does reading become an integral part of sadhana. Otherwise mere reading is irrelevant to spiritual progress. We have known so many professors, learned people discussing the fine points of Advaita and the like, of Shankara, Ramanuja; men like Kant, Hegel, Russell discussing many more fine points, but are they spiritual? They are not. They are mental. Their lives may well be unspiritual. If you stop with reading, if you are satisfied with it and do not make an effort to make it a living knowledge, you are a prisoner of what you read. And that is another trap. When you read, when you study, you have to see how it can influence your life. Each reading must be a step forward in changing the quality of your life.

For instance: if there be a quarrel with somebody today, do not remember that quarrel when you meet that person tomorrow. Give him a chance, that person may have changed. He may be different another day.

Now this is a very beautiful idea, one feels very nice when one reads it, but am I going to follow it tomorrow? If somebody insults me today, and I have occasion to meet him tomorrow, will I forget today's insult? If I do not, what I have read has no value. It remains in the theory drawer of my mind.

Thus reading has to be constructively utilised to better my life. There must be a balance between my study and my activity. What I read must be integrated with the rest of my life. Reading by itself becomes an obsession and works as a trap.

II

RITUALS — EMOTIONS — PSYCHIC

We were speaking of pitfalls in sadhana. Let us be clear that pitfalls are different from downfalls. When there is a downfall there is no mistaking it. The person who is affected knows it, everybody else knows it too. But in pitfalls, the danger is, the person concerned may not often realise that he is in a pit. Very frequently he thinks he is in a very high state, that he is doing something great. In the Indian mythology there is a story of Lord Vishnu taking the form of a pig and wallowing in the gutter; he would not return to his Vaikuntha. When Narada comes to him to remind, he says he is happy where he is. It takes quite a while for Narada to make Vishnu aware of the state he is in and he is ready to go back.

So pitfalls are very deceptive. One does not know that one has got stuck in a pit. Illustratively, we spoke of how work can become a prison. Without fulfilling the conditions of detachment, disinterested offering, elimination of the motive-force of ego and desire, work becomes an obsession and one is apt to bulldoze through the collectivity hurting others, disregarding others, developing one's self-importance, in all ways becoming very unspiritual. Such work loses its spiritual character. But the person involved may not know that he is acting that way; he tends to feel that others lack the spiritual perspective to appreciate him.

Then we went on to consider the question of reading literature, books, scriptures, shastras and saw how reading, which is intended to enlarge the mind, broaden the consciousness, can become something narrowing, limiting and we can lose sight of the purpose for which we study. We tend to limit ourselves to a particular philosophy, a particular doctrine and shut our eyes to what else may be there. Mother used to recollect how her brother, when he was 16 or 17, was once crossing a bridge over the River Seine at night when he heard a voice say very clearly, "Do you want to become a god?" He started and said, "No, I want to help humanity." And Mother says he had his way. He went to Africa, became the Governor-General and helped the backward races, but he lost the destiny that was offered to him. And that was because his mind had become narrow. To help others, help humanity, that had become his obsession; humanism blinded him to greater pursuits.

Indeed you must have a central knowledge but you cannot shut your mind to other vistas of knowledge. Knowledge grows, knowledge is never static. You should always be ready to look at the other's point of view. It will not do to condemn without knowing what you are condemning. Sri Aurobindo even goes to the extent of saying that it is a sign of wisdom when you not only have knowledge of a thing but are also prepared to acknowledge that the opposite also can be true in its own conditions. Now this shows the broadness of mind, a fragment of which at least, we can assimilate: to know that there must be some truth behind what we may not agree with, what we may not accept. That truth may be relevant to certain people, to some order of humanity. You must have a plastic mind and even a pragmatic one. You must be always ready to apply your knowledge to your life-situations and cast your daily life in its mould. Otherwise you shut yourself in a box and preen yourself on your possessions — ultimately at your cost.

Another common pitfall is *rituals*, *bhajans*, *ceremonial worship*. When these were started in every religion there was a significance and symbolic value. They were intended to awaken the senses, the outgoing faculties towards some higher reality. Gradually the inner significance was lost and people started paying attention to the little, minute details of the ceremonial pageant, — the way the flowers are arranged, the way the lamps are lit, the way the *āratis* are done, the way the idols are kept etc. All energy, all attention was centred on surface details and on repeating the formulae. Now most of us do not indulge in these rituals but the external aspect of paying homage, a kind of worship, affirming our adoration, that itself can become very mechanical. And we may be very satisfied that we have done something. We begin to go through the ritual mechanically, even wrongly, e.g. when some people turn the lighted joss-sticks anti-clockwise. Without being conscious we may be drawn into repetitions of such mechanical movements. When the external aspect preponderates, our mind may be elsewhere, it may be busy with something else while the hand goes on moving. Rituals have value only when they are done with full awareness and attention; otherwise they turn into a trap.

Similarly bhajans, music as an aid to raise the finer emotions towards God; that is the purpose but instead of being spiritual movements, movements of the soul, very often they tend to become vital movements. That is why bhajans as such were not encouraged here because the participants in bhajans, as they go on, turn it into vital movements; they enjoy the vital swing, they enjoy the surge of vital emotions. The rush of tears is cathartic to begin with, but at some point there is the danger of public display of these emotions. These manifestations of excitement are often mistaken for spiritual inspiration, spiritual intimacy. And then there is dancing. I had thought that they were our special contribution from India, but when I visited the West, I saw they too have their share in these dramatic turns of finer emotions. For hours together they would dance; somebody would beat drums, some would have drugs and it would go on and on. Now a spiritual dance is never made to order. It is a spontaneous play of movements which correspond to an inner change of consciousness. But how many of us are conscious of this impulsion? This danger of vital movements being mistaken for spiritual movements is very much present in ritual dances, collective bhajans, public worship.

Japa is a very effective and potent means but when it is done mechanically, when the mind roves but you go on telling the beads it is a fruitless exercise. To concentrate on numbers, one lakh, two lakhs, three lakhs etc. becomes mechanical. The purpose of communion with God, communication of your emotions and prayers to God, is forgotten. That is why, Patanjali, the master of yoga says: *tad japah tadartha bhāvanam*, that is japa where you dwell on the meaning; you are conscious of what you utter, Om Anandamayi, Chaitanyamayi, Satyamayi, Parame: each time you pronounce Anandamayi, you feel how she is full of ananda; Chaitanyamayi, how she is full of consciousness and so on. It does not matter if you do it three times or seven times, you need not do a hundred times, but it has to be a living japa. The moment you allow the external mechanism to take possession, you lose contact.

Speaking of emotions, it is very important to note that in the chest there is a place where there is a surge of emotions, good or bad, or what the tantrics call the *anāhata chakra* and what Sri Aurobindo calls the emotional centre. When there is a movement of love, movement of prayer, surrender at the emotional level, men often think it is a psychic movement; there are many who tell you that their psychic is active. But to attain the psychic is a very great achievement. It is a capital step which cannot be easily arrived at. Mother used to say that it takes nearly thirty years for an earnest seeker to get the psychic realisation. But, perhaps seeing the effect that her statement had on all of us, she said that it is not so in everybody's case; there is the Grace, one may be ready and it can come any time. But the message went home. We have to do homework, we have to satisfy the conditions of psychic realisation. Psychic feeling is different, psychic experience is different, psychic realisation is different. Psychicisation is still more different. It does not come so easily. When there is the feeling of love, which is the character of the psychic, we must really examine ourselves to see whether it is a mixture, whether it is self-referring or other-referring, whether it is something that has nothing to do with our selfish ego, our demands, our desires and is a spontaneous movement of self-giving. If it is that without reference to the subject, irrespective of whether it is recognised or not, then it is the result of a wave from the psychic. Note that the psychic being is behind the emotional centre. Most of us have not even cleansed our emotional being. Our emotional being is a sea of mixed, turbid emotions, waves of positive and negative emotions. We have to first sift the negative ones from the positive ones, stabilise the positive ones and then use that as a spring-board to go deeper to feel the psychic in itself. This is another tempting mistake that many do in taking the emotional centre for the psychic centre.

In all our movements there has to be a sense of proportion. The sense of proportion is the beginning of what is called beauty in aesthetics. Beauty is the right proportion of everything, all elements justly combined to produce a harmonious whole. What is normally mistaken for beauty is attraction, anything that strikes the eye, but the secret of beauty is something deeper. It does not lie in colour, it does not lie in form but in the consciousness that vibrates in a thing and for that we must have a sense of proportion. Everything has its place, anything out of place is discordant.

That has been the ruin of India in following the path of asceticism. All the God-given beauty, all the joy and harmony of Nature is rejected, thrown aside and ugliness is given a premium. Barrenness, ugliness, denial — denial of food, denial of apparel, denial of sleep — self-denial is lauded and the ego preens itself over it. But this kind of denial of the things that should be accepted, organised and beautified, leads to a false sense of self-importance and fattening of the ego. Asceticism for its own sake is again another trap. Mother says: "Be a saint without appearing to be a saint." When you want to appear a saint, it is a falsehood. Why do you need the appurtenances of sainthood? Be natural to your state of being, state of consciousness. This sense of superiority based on self-denial has been the ruin of many spiritually promising people. The Gita speaks of asuric tapas. Beware of it.

The sense of elitism that I am superior, my teaching is the highest, my teacher is the one avatar, has been the curse of many seekers or even movements. Some are foolish enough to show this one-upmanship, some are clever enough to conceal it. But their attitude towards the commonalty is highly unspiritual. The Jews have paid for centuries for this sense of elitism. Brahminism in India has been paying for it dearly. This false sense of superiority, spirit of elitism has been the ruin of many collectivities.

And it is most inexcusable in a spiritual community. People who are rich may have their ego of wealth; they are very patronising, they are philanthropic because they enjoy lording it over others through their charity, wanting people to feel grateful to them. That is another kind of elitism which cancels whatever good karma their deeds may forge. Economic elitism, political elitism, scientific elitism are some other types, we do not speak of them here. We are concerned with spiritual elitism which is the most inexcusable because spirituality itself requires a basic attitude of equality, oneness with all. The moment we start feeling superior, higher than others, that is the end of spirituality. So we need to remind ourselves of this frailty because, as I have noted elsewhere, wherever I have been in different countries, people have not lost an opportunity to tell me that we here have an insufferable sense of elitism. Even the most ignorant person has this sense of superiority over the rest. This is a very big pitfall. Whenever you feel superior to others, that you have something which others do not have, please think twice, examine yourself once again why the feeling has come. Do not forget you are in somebody's boat.

Speaking of the psychic I pointed out the common mistake of taking the emotional for the psychic. The psychic itself is deep inside in the cave of the heart. There are beautiful descriptions in the Upanishads, in Mother's utterances. Sri Aurobindo has left no room for doubt in his very precise definitions. Now, the fount of love is in the psychic, the nature of the psychic expression must be one of harmony, beauty, joy. Whenever we touch it even for a second, we feel the world to be something different. There is an outflow of unself-regarding love towards all. That is a promise, an assurance that you are capable of Love. But a lot of homework has to be done before that becomes more frequent, becomes a permanent factor in life. That needs expression in our human relations. Our love cannot be a matter between ourselves and God alone. Remember Sri Aurobindo saying that your love for God is incomplete unless you love God in all. So this love has to flow out and you have to express it in your relations with everyone around, with your colleagues, with relatives, with your students, with your servants, with everybody. You must learn to function from that basis. You can no longer be self-centred. A mental belief that you are equal to all is not enough. It has to come spontaneously. Human relations are the field where you prepare the ground for the psychic climate. A psychic climate has to be built up, made natural, before the psychic can emerge forward again and again and influence our life. For that one has to denude oneself of all that is unpsychic, of all that is rough, ugly, of all that is mean and selfish. If Mother disliked any particular quality in human beings, it was selfishness. We tend to justify it in some form or other. It is inexcusable, whether it is spiritual selfishness or a social selfishness, it is all the same from a higher level. Selfishness has to go and selflessness has to take its place. It is only when this preparation has gone far enough, when the ego-self is given the go-by, that the true Self can be induced to come forward. Otherwise the psychic elements get mixed up and misused and exploited by the ego for its own aggrandisement.

III

OBSESSIONS — DEFECTS — DESIRES

We observed that the first pitfall is mistaking the means for the end. What is a process, a way, tends to be confused with the goal. We saw how without the right attitude, work becomes labour, reading becomes learning and rituals become an obsession. We observed that everywhere we must keep a sense of proportion and we warned ourselves against the danger of ego, including the spiritual ego, which borders on elitism. We noted also the common mistake of confusing the emotional centre with the psychic which is deep within.

Next we come to detachment. It has been a watchword of all disciplines of yoga, all lines of sadhana. We must not be attached, we must be detached; we are asked to cultivate a stern detachment from people, relationships, objects, habits. A very wise counsel, no doubt, but in the process of detaching ourselves, we often slip into a more dangerous alley. Very religiously we practise detachment from people around us: ostentatiously we cut off family relations, worldly relations and friendships. We escape from our responsibilities, duties, under the plea of getting detached.

But that is not the end of the story. While detaching ourselves from others, many of us develop attachment to our own selves. "My views, my habits, my preferences, my assessments, my needs", — to these we attach too much importance, because the normal avenues of occupation of serving others, of pouring our energies for others, are closed to us and those energies are diverted to ourselves. This attachment to ourselves becomes inordinate. I develop attachment to everything about me. If I give up my family relations, if I refuse to meet them, if I refuse to attend to their letters, I devote double time for cleaning my bicycle, for cleaning my shaving blade. Now, this involvement with myself is a typical pitfall in the process of getting detached from others. Our detachment from others is not genuine, it is often a cover for selfishness, for selfish pursuits of my own interests. And in this attachment to myself, to my ways of living and my so-called needs, I develop obsessions.

In the absence of family responsibilities, one tends to develop some time-consuming habits, viz. cleanliness, neatness. One washes hands ten times, four times with soap, three times with cold water, then wipe three times. This becomes an obsession. Care of books is another compulsive pastime. One does not get satisfaction till one takes out each book every day and dusts it. So much of time, so much of energy, is being spent on these things. Small elemental beings, mischievous forces take advantage of such situations to ride over you, to sit on your back and point out, 'you have not done this, you have not done that, you have not cleaned this.' We have known of people having nervous breakdowns because of such obsessions. You shave yourself, the blade needs to be used four times on one side and four times on the other. In the middle you forget whether you have done it thrice or twice. Once again it starts. You become a prisoner of an alien agency. So this obsession with cleanliness is an exaggerated preoccupation, which totally removes you from the path of sadhana. I have known a person who, when he discovered that he was becoming a victim to this habit, deliberately cultivated the opposite habit, of living with dust, of letting books gather dust, sitting on a chair with dust, without dusting it, till he became indifferent. That was the only way he could escape from the clutches of this kind of obsession.

Similarly, people who diet: they give such excessive importance to these things that, instead of the divine consciousness, they are full of calorie-consciousness. Their mind always dwells on that. These are illustrative of the petty little obsessions that develop into huge dangers swallowing up all your time. So, next time anything of this type happens, please remember that this is a kind of possession by the lower forces who try to hold you and restrain you from proceeding further in your sadhana. Nothing should become an obsession, in everything there should be a balance, there must be a sense of proportion. Nobody asks us to live in a shabby way. Decent cleanliness, a balanced neatness, but not an obsessive cleanliness. That becomes a disease. Rituals, habits, should never be allowed to take possession of us. They are meant for our living. We are not meant for them. This is to be kept in mind. Never become a prisoner of habits, of conventions, of obsessions.

Speaking of detachment, it is enough if, whenever you do a thing or are asked to do a thing, you do not get involved personally. Do to your best capacity, not perfunctorily, do it as well as you can but do not lose yourself totally in it. If you lose yourself in any work totally, involve yourself completely, you are lost. The witness-position, what Mother calls stepping-back, stepping back and watching, is lost. Some portion of your being must be always aloof, aloof enough to observe, 'Am I doing the right thing, have I spoken the right words, am I reacting in the right way?' You cannot do that if you are totally involved. Something must always be above, above your nature, above the mind and vital, because when you are so above, you are nearer the soul, nearer the Self. This tact of doing things well, but at the same time keeping something of yourself above the movement, observing it, must be cultivated.

It is a very very common weakness to dwell too much on one's defects. All human beings have plus points and minus points. Observe your weak points, observe your defects, but do not dwell upon them too much. Note, make up your mind to get over them. But to dwell upon them, to always think of them, to let them overpower you, make you feel small — well, that is to play into the hands of the wrong forces by indulging in them negatively. What happened ten years ago, what happened when you behaved badly with someone, all these things have a way of confronting you when you feel nice, peaceful. From where do they come? You can say they come from the subconscient, where they were waiting, as it were. Things which happened twenty years ago suddenly come alive. Somebody wrote the other day in a very picturesque language how he was taught to meditate. Well, summoning all his devotion, he sat near his God's portrait and he had a very warm feeling. Suddenly he started weeping bitterly. Now what happened? Some thought it was out of devotion, an emotional outburst, but no. All the wrong things, or allegedly wrong, that he had done in his life crowded before his mind's eye, making him feel guilty; he realised he had been mean, lamentably selfish and was struck with remorse. He wept uncontrollably. After that, of course, he had some relief. But if you let such things repeat themselves, they will haunt you all the time. So do not dwell too much on defects. The past is past, do not allow the negative past to interfere with your progress into the future. Even the present should not be vitiated by such remembrance of the past. The past should be remembered just enough to keep you from repeating past wrongs.

It is understood that none of us here believes any longer in the superstitions of punishments and rewards. God does not punish. It is we who punish ourselves. God does not reward. It is our karmic reactions. It is in our hands to try to atone for the past wrongs,— whether it is a moral wrong, or a spiritual or a social one. Again and again recalling it and feeling sorry for it is not the way. Mother pointedly says that once you feel sorry, once you make up your mind that it will not happen again, that is enough. That is enough atonement, that cancels the karma. Only you must be sincere in not allowing it to happen again. So, do not dwell too much on defects, to do so is a negative indulgence. Instead of a positive indulgence which we all recognise, it is a negative exercise whose real character is concealed.

And last about surrender. Surrender is a big word. It contains a whole life-time of sadhana in itself. But what we understand normally by surrender is the decision to leave everything to the Divine. Crudely, this concept of surrender has been understood as surrender of physical possessions. Whatever resources one has, one gives it all to God or to one who represents God. But this does not always end there, as it should. Slowly a claim sets in, albeit unconsciously: the person feels that having surrendered, it is the responsibility of the Divine to attend to him. It is an implicit claim. But this external surrender, Sri Aurobindo points out, is only symbolic, only a sign of readiness to give what you have and are to the Divine. It has to be worked out in detail. External possessions are not very difficult to give, but it is the internal possessions, habits, preferences, desires, emotions, that are more difficult to surrender. They have to be surrendered one by one. They cannot be surrendered in a lump. This detailed working out of surrender in life is consecration. In thoughts, in feelings, in actions, at every step to consider: is this consistent with the higher will of God? Tune your will to that, surrender your choice at every moment to that will. That is surrender, and it requires a long long time to work it out in one's self on all planes of the being.

Desires are to be surrendered. Sri Aurobindo speaks of pulling out desire from its bleeding roots. Each desire that is pulled out leaves a painful feeling of regret in the vital. But desire has to be rejected. Here again we conveniently deceive ourselves by confusing desires with needs. We say it is a need, not a desire. Now who is to decide what is a need, what is a desire? Many have put this question to the Mother. The central point is that if a need, a genuine need, is there and it is submitted to the Divine, it is always granted. If it is not granted, take it that it is not your real need. It is only a seeming need. A desire, if it is not fulfilled, leaves a lot of agitation, disappointment, frustration, but a need does not, because when it is a real need you are content to wait, saying that He knows the hour, He knows whether you really need it or not.

These are some of the pitfalls that are fairly common among most of the sadhanas and we can never be too much warned against them. If our last three sessions have awakened some sense of vigilance against these possibilities, I would think our labours have been sufficiently rewarded.